THE WEAPONS ENCYCLOPÆDIA
TANK AIRCRAFT AFV SHIP ARTILLERY VEHICLES SECRET WEAPON

TWE-027 ENG

AUTOBLINDO AB40/41/42/43

THE WEAPONS ENCYCLOPAEDIA

EDITORIAL STAFF
Luca Cristini, Paolo Crippa.

ACADEMIC STAFF
Enrico Acerbi, Massimiliano Afiero, Aldo Antonicelli, Ruggero Calò, Luigi Carretta, Flavio Chistè, Anna Cristini, Carlo Cucut, Salvo Fagone, Enrico Finazzer, Arturo Giusti, Björn Huber, Andrea Lombardi, Aymeric Lopez, Marco Lucchetti, Gabriele Malavoglia, Luigi Manes, Giovanni Maressi, Francesco Mattesini, Daniele Notaro, Péter Mujzer, Federico Peirani, Alberto Peruffo, Maurizio Raggi, Andrea Alberto Tallillo, Antonio Tallillo, Roberto Vela, Massimo Zorza.

PUBLISHED BY
Luca Cristini Editore (Soldiershop), via Orio, 35/4 - 24050 Zanica (BG) ITALY.

DISTRIBUTION BY
Soldiershop - www.soldiershop.com, Amazon, Ingram Spark, Berliner Zinnfigurem (D), LaFeltrinelli, Mondadori, Libera Editorial (Spain), Google book (eBook), Kobo, (eBoook), Apple Book (eBook).

PUBLISHING'S NOTES
None of unpublished images or text of our book may be reproduced in any format without the expressed written permission of Luca Cristini Editore (already Soldiershop.com) when not indicate as marked with license creative commons 3.0 or 4.0. Luca Cristini Editore has made every reasonable effort to locate, contact and acknowledge rights holders and to correctly apply terms and conditions to Content. Every effort has been made to trace the copyright of all the photographs. If there are unintentional omissions, please contact the publisher in writing at: info@soldiershop.com, who will correct all subsequent editions.

LICENSES COMMONS
This book may utilize part of material marked with license creative commons 3.0 or 4.0 (CC BY 4.0), (CC BY-ND 4.0), (CC BY-SA 4.0) or (CC0 1.0). We give appropriate attribution credit and indicate if change were made in the acknowledgments field. Our WTW books series utilize only fonts licensed under the SIL Open Font License or other free use license.

CONTRIBUTORS OF THIS VOLUME & ACKNOWLEDGEMENTS
We would like to thank the main contributors to this issue: The profiles of the floats are all by the author. The colouring of the photos is by Anna Cristini. Special thanks to national and/or private institutions such as: Army General Staff, State Archives, Bundesarchiv, Nara, Library of Congress, Wikipedia, USAF, Signal magazine, War Chronicles, War Front, IWM, Australian War Museum, etc. A P.Crippa, A.Lopez, Péter Mujzer, L.Manes, C.Cucut, Tallillo archives. Model Victoria (www.modelvictoria.it) etc. for providing images or other items from their archives.

For a complete list of Soldiershop titles, or for every information please contact us on our website: www.soldiershop.com or www.cristinieditore.com. E-mail: info@soldiershop.com. Keep up to date on Facebook https://www.facebook.com/soldiershop.publishing

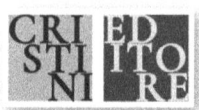

Title: **AUTOBLINDO AB40/41/42/43** Code.: **TWE-027 EN**
Series by L. S. Cristini
ISBN code: 979125589XXXX First edition July 2024
THE WEAPONS ENCYCLOPAEDIA (SOLDIERSHOP) is a trademark of Luca Cristini Editore

THE WEAPONS ENCYCLOPÆDIA
TANK AIRCRAFT AFV SHIP ARTILLERY VEHICLES SECRET WEAPON

AUTOBLINDO AB40/41/42/43

LUCA STEFANO CRISTINI

BOOK SERIES FOR MODELERS & COLLECTORS

CONTENTS

Autoblindo FIAT-Ansaldo AB .... pag. 5
- Development .... pag. 5
- Technical features .... pag. 6

Versions of the vehicle .... pag. 15
- AB40 .... pag. 15
- Development .... pag. 15
- Armament .... pag. 16
- AB42 .... pag. 18
- AB with 47/32 cannon and railway .... pag. 18

AB41 and 43 .... pag. 23

Operational use .... pag. 31

Camouflage and distinctive signs .... pag. 49

Production and export .... pag. 55

Data sheet .... pag. 57

Bibliography .... pag. 58

▲ Nice photo of an Autoblindo AB43 taken in the exhibition park in Novegro by the author. Interesting for the camouflage and many other details

AUTOBLINDO FIAT ANSALDO AB

In the period between the First and Second World Wars, despite the excellent results achieved during, firstly, the reconquest of Libya and then in the Ethiopian War of 1935, with armoured cars left over from the Great War, the development of such vehicles in our country was shelved in favour of light tanks. However, this approach began to be revised for two main reasons:

- The long-range patrolling needs of the Italian African Police emerged with the huge colonial expansion;
- The need for vehicles adapted to the new large armoured units, to equip the scout units.

In light of the specifications requested by both the Cavalry and the P.A.I., the Ministry of War decided in 1937 to initiate a request for a single model of 'armoured car' with high performance in terms of protection, mobility in all terrain and autonomy. The note also specified that the prototype should be available by 1939.

Among the first to respond to the request was SPA Ansaldo Fossati, which designed a vehicle with the following characteristics:
- traction on all four wheels;
- rear engine;
- Main armament consisting of two 8mm machine guns in a revolving turret;
- secondary armament with an 8mm machine gun in the rear of the fighting compartment;
- possibility of driving both forwards and backwards, as was already the case with the Lancia 1Z.

The two prototypes, one for the Army and one for the P.A.I., were officially presented in the spring of 1939. The new armoured car was approved in March 1940 as the 'Autoblindo 40' and an initial batch of 176 was ordered. However, the first five vehicles were only delivered to the Armoured Car Training Centre of the Pinerolo Cavalry School in March 1941.

In the meantime, once the order had been received, it was decided to replace the main armament, consisting of two Breda Mod. 38 8mm machine guns, with a 20mm M35 piece from Breda, which was much better performing and capable of firing armour-piercing and high-explosive ammunition. This was combined with a single Breda Mod. 38 machine gun, while the secondary armament remained unchanged. After these initial improvements in 1941, the vehicle was renamed AB 41, a version that was later also the best known and most widespread.

The only armoured cars that were definitely delivered with the initial turret armed with 8mm Breda machine guns were probably the first five units destined for the Pinerolo Cavalry School and, later, the first batch of railway armoured cars.

As already mentioned, the AB 41, unlike most of the vehicles developed during the conflict, was one of the most successful and modern Italian military vehicles. It was very successful, equipped with innovative solutions such as dual guidance and the use of the two external spare wheels as 'crazy wheels', useful when overcoming obstacles. The range was also remarkable, more than double that of other Italian armoured vehicles, and the suspension system was state-of-the-art. The only flaws, according to some veterans, were the usual weak bolt-on plate armour which, added to the shoddy materials often used, tended to fracture or crack after violent impacts, and some minor problems reported by its crews with the steering system, which were never fully resolved.

In total, over 700 units of the AB 40, AB 41 and AB 43 versions were built (the AB 42 was only made as a prototype version), including over 100 produced during the German occupation, some of which remained in service even after the end of the conflict until the early 1950s.

■ DEVELOPMENT

The development of the Fiat Ansaldo armoured car began in 1938. In that year, but also earlier, there was a clear need for a new vehicle to be used in the colonies by the PAI (Polizia dell'Africa Italiana). This request was in addition to a similar one from the Royal Army for a cavalry vehicle to replace the old Lancia IZs. For the first prototype, the chassis with independent suspension and four-wheel steering that had already been developed for the Fiat-SPA TM40 artillery tractor was used. The hull consisted of ballistic plates bolted onto the chassis.

With a view to its use as a reconnaissance vehicle, the armoured car was equipped with dual controls, allowing the vehicle to move either forwards or backwards. With one driving position at the front and one at the rear, this allowed the direction of travel to be quickly reversed. Another distinctive feature of the vehicle, and one that distinguished its design, were the two spare wheels housed halfway up the side; these wheels, placed in neutral, acted as an aid to overcoming obstacles when driving off-road.

TECHNICAL FEATURES

Engine and suspension

The engine in the AB40 version armed with a Model 1941 turret was a FIAT SPA ABM 1 6-cylinder in-line water-cooled 78 hp, while in the standard AB41 it was a FIAT-SPA ABM 2 6-cylinder in-line 88 hp. petrol engine cooled by a water circuit driven by a centrifugal pump. The engine cooling water tank was located under the rear driver's door, to the left of the fuel reserve tank. In both ABs, the engine was coupled to a Zenith type 42 TTVP carburettor housed in the rear of the engine compartment. Both engines were produced by SPA on behalf of FIAT. This engine, especially the second one, allowed the vehicle to reach the good speed of 76km per hour on the road.

Armour

The armouring of the entire hull and superstructure of the first armoured car to be named AB40 consisted of bolted plates. This arrangement did not offer the same efficiency as a mechanically welded plate but facilitated the replacement of an armour element should it need to be repaired. The hull had a somewhat light thickness of only 9 mm, located on the front, sides and rear bodywork, while the turret, which was more heavily reinforced, reached a maximum thickness of 40 mm on the front plate and 30 mm on the sides and rear. The wheel guards were also armoured to prevent enemy fire from piercing the tyres.

In general, for the tasks the armoured car had to perform, the armour was more than adequate, protecting the crew from the light weapons of the enemy infantry.

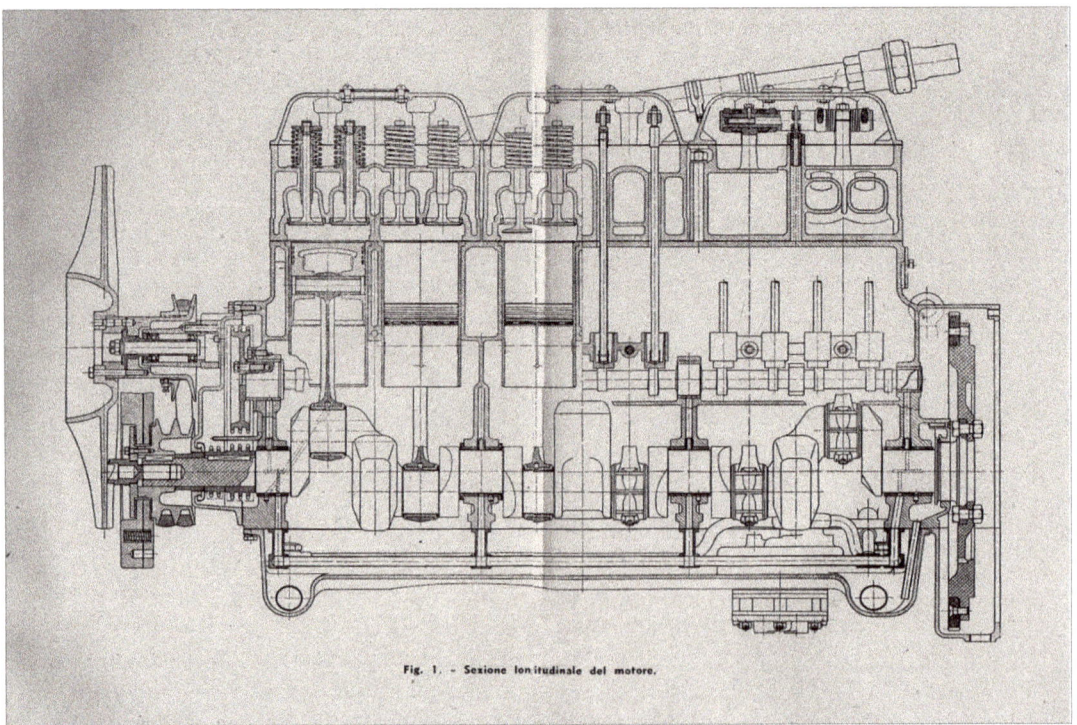

▲ Longitudinal section of the engine, from the original owner's manual. Author collection.

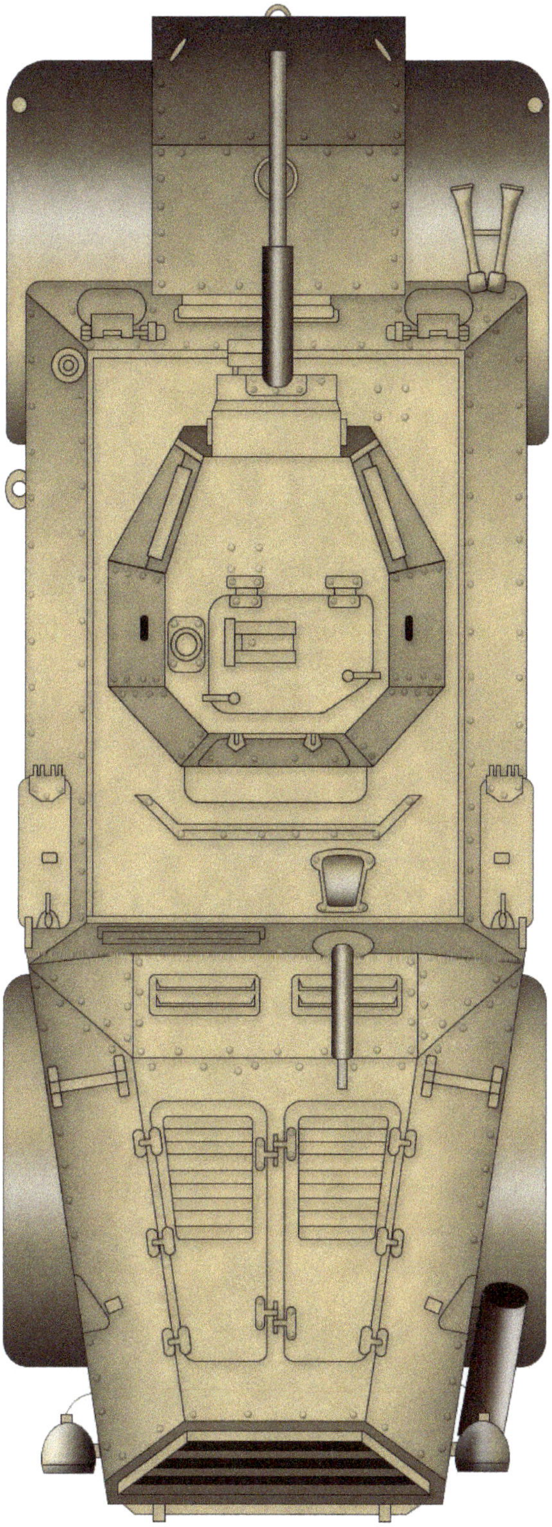

▲ AB41 armoured car profile from above.

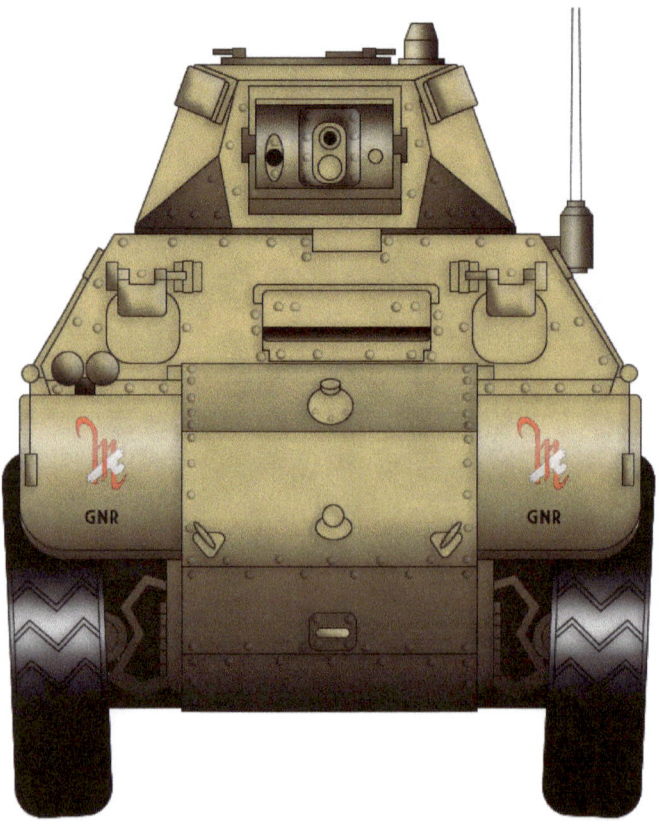

▲ AB41 armoured car profile front and rear view.

AUTOBLINDO AB40 A.O.I. 1940

▲ AB40 in the forces of the colonial police units in Africa. The camouflage colouring at the time was similar to that of the M11/39 tanks and the L3 light tanks presented by FIAT in those years.

AUTOBLINDO AB40 IN LIBYA, DECEMBER 1940

▲ AB40 armoured car in North Africa. One of the very first colonial units equipped with this vehicle. It was soon replaced by the more powerful AB41 and all the old machines were immediately converted to the new model.

The hull of the armoured car had an internal structure onto which the plates were bolted. At the rear of the superstructure were the two armoured access doors, divided into two parts that could be opened separately. The upper part had a slot so that the crew could use their personal weapons for close defence. To the left was the antenna, which rested on a bracket at the rear of the superstructure. In fact, to open the top of the left door, it was necessary to raise the antenna a few degrees.

On the right side the horn was positioned at the front, on the right side there was a pick and the exhaust pipe was positioned on the rear wing. The two spare wheels were located in two fairings on either side of the superstructure. In the 'Railway' version, the support in the fairing allowed two wheels to be attached on each side. Above the engine compartment were two air intakes and two hatches for engine maintenance. At the rear were the cooling grille and the two rear lights.

Radio system

We do not know which radio models were mounted on the ABs before 1941. We do know that from March of that year, a model RF 3M transceiver station, manufactured by Magneti Marelli, was installed on the armoured cars. This equipment was positioned on the left wall of the superstructure, in the centre of the crew compartment. The RF 3M consisted of a transmitter placed on a shelf above the receiver, which in turn was placed on another shelf on the spare wheel fairing. Underneath were the power supplies and accumulator on the floor, while the batteries were concealed in the double bottom of the floor. There were two pairs of headphones and

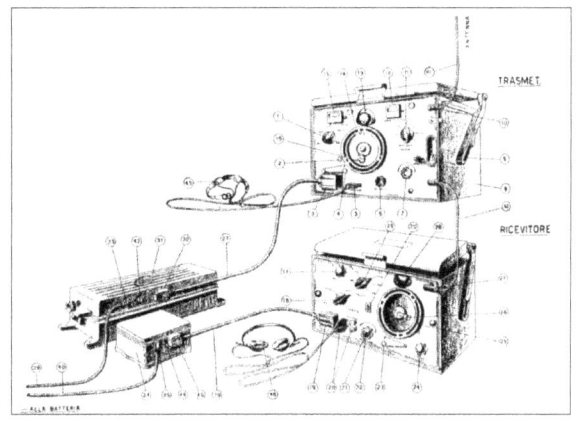

▶ Radio system diagram of the AB, from the original user manual. Author Collection.

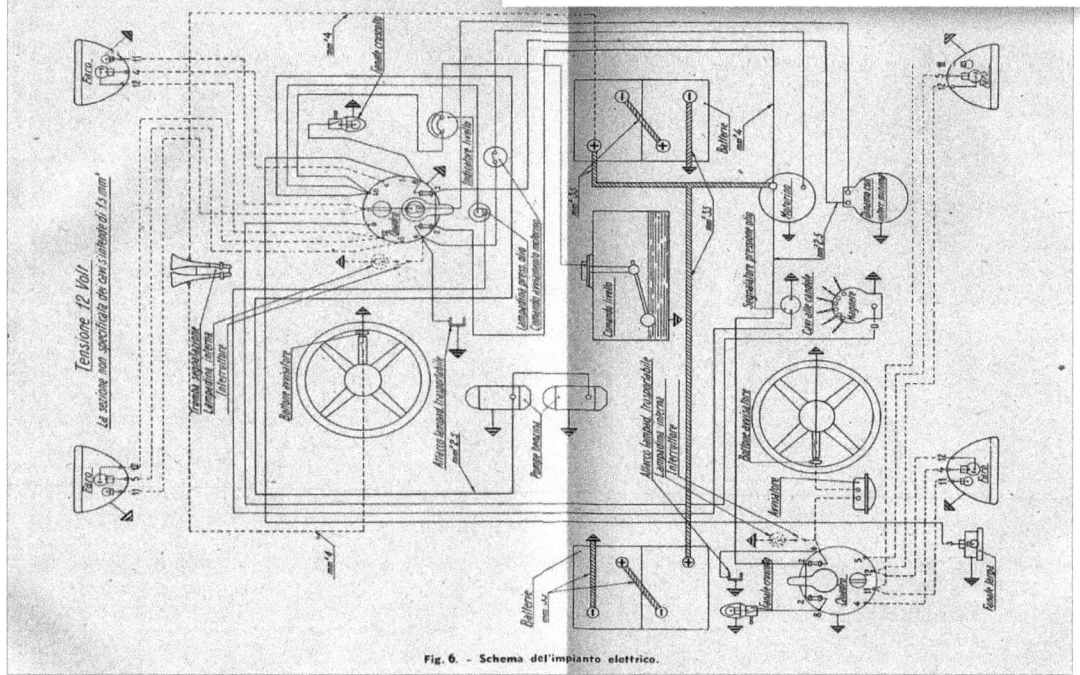

▲ Diagram of the AB armoured car electrical system. From the original owner's manual. Author's collection.

AUTOBLINDO AB41, NORTHERN AFRICA 1940

▲ AB41 armoured car in Libya. Belonging to the II Armoured Squadron Group 'Novara'. The Group was provided with this vehicle to replace the L6/40 lost in battle. As with the light tanks, the ABs also bore the stylised 1920 coat of arms on the front of the vehicle.

microphones for the intercom, one used by the front pilot and the second by the rear gunner. The externally mounted antenna could be folded down to 90°. When raised, it could reach a height of three metres and up to seven when fully extended. This maximum aperture gave it a range of 60 km and 25/35 km if placed at 3 m height. Some armoured cars received an RF 2CA radio, also manufactured by Magneti Marelli, with the antenna mounted on the rear of the combat compartment, but apart from the antenna mount, there were no external differences between the normal AB41 and the command version. The RF 2CA was used for communications between tank squadron commanders; therefore, it is logical to assume that AB41s equipped with this type of radio were used by squadron/company commanders.

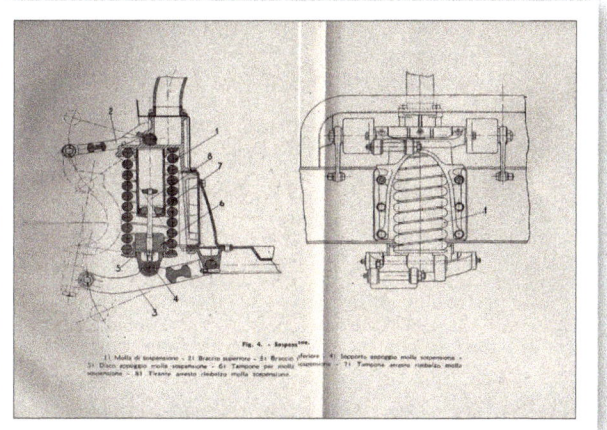

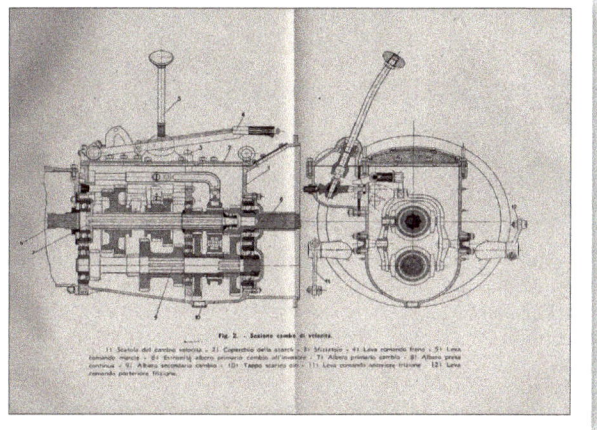

▶ Above, small picture: the wheel suspension system of the AB armoured cars.

Below: diagram of the AB's engine gearbox system. From the original owner's manual. Author collection.

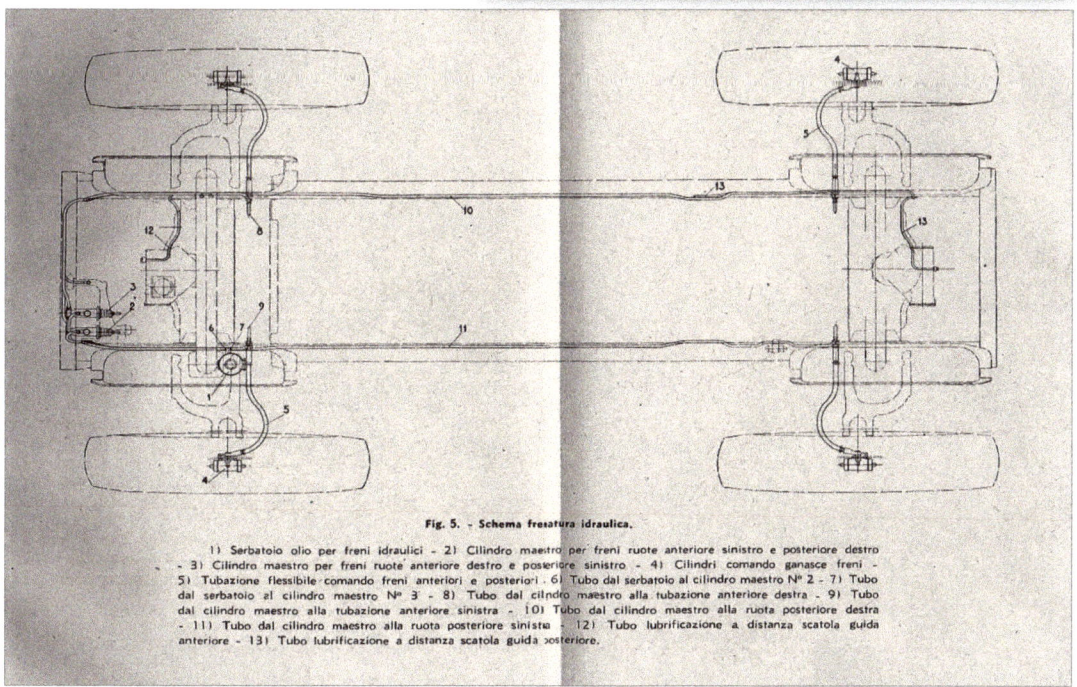

▲ Diagram of the AB armoured car braking system. From the original owner's manual. Author Collection.

▲ An AB40 used at the cavalry training school in Pinerolo.

▼ An AB40 with Pirelli 'Artiglio' tyres of the first type. The Breda 38 machine gun mounted on the rear of the vehicle was dismantled and placed in the anti-aircraft gun mount. Slits are visible on the door and the regimental badge can be seen next to it.

VERSIONS OF THE VEHICLE

AB40

The first AB Ansaldo-class Autoblindo was the AB40, of which a total of 24 were produced with the first model 40 turret. Another 435 prepared as 40s were instead converted into AB41s.
The prototype was built by FIAT and Ansaldo, who worked together on the project
An initial wooden model was then built and presented to the officers of the Army General Staff during a visit to the Ansaldo factory in Genoa on 11 April 1938. From the prototype, the model was very similar to the final vehicle, with four-wheel drive, four steering wheels with independent suspension, a petrol engine, armament consisting of three 8 mm machine guns and four crew members.

DEVELOPMENT

The first wooden model was soon followed in May 1939 by two prototypes of the armoured car, which in its early days was called the Armoured Car (ABM) (Ing: Machine gun Armored Car).
Compared to the final version in the following months and years there were some differences. Starting with the headlights, which were not yet in the fairings inside the superstructure, and the maintenance flaps on the engine bonnet had no air intakes. The PAI version also had a large hole placed above the turret, and had a vertical radio antenna fixed to the front right of the superstructure, as well as a siren placed on the rear of the hull and an armoured plate covering the spare wheels. After the General Staff, the vehicle was seen by the Duce himself. Mussolini was favourably impressed by the new vehicle, especially by its elegant lines.
Compared to the first prototype, the final one had air intakes on the engine deck and all the headlights were fitted with armour. In the light of so much enthusiasm, the vehicle was tested operationally.
The test vehicle was sent to Italian East Africa. It landed at Massawa in Eritrea on 3 June 1939. From there it set off on a test tour of over 13,000 km, returning to Massawa on 12 September. Despite the difficult weather conditions, the armoured car completed the test, which was considered a success. Observations during the test suggested the following improvements: the addition of an anti-aircraft machine gun mount on the turret, the replacement of the huge fixed searchlight on the turret with a smaller one that could be manoeuvred by the commander, the installation of a system that allowed the radio antenna to be folded down on the right side of the superstructure and the removal of the spare wheel guard (only provided for the PAI version). Further tests followed, again in Africa, but this time in Libya. What became apparent as a flaw on this occasion was the armament, consisting of three medium machine guns, which did not prove suitable for infantry support, however urgency and military requirements forced production to start anyway,

▲ AB40 in service with the PAI East Africa Police. Note the large beacon on the turret and the antenna on the front.

while FIAT and Ansaldo engineers developed a new version that would become the more famous AB41! Meanwhile, after receiving all these initial modifications (armament aside), the AutoBlindo Mod. 1940 or AB40 (Autoblindota Mod. 1940) was officially born on 18 March 1940.

The final version of the AB40, badged RE 116B. It is distinguished from previous vehicles by the absence of the large headlight on the turret, the elimination of the two rear air intakes on the turret, the adoption of new wheel rims and the addition of a Notek headlight on the front of the superstructure. The front mudguards were shortened while a second horn was added on the right front mudguard. Production was then started, beginning in January 1941 with the first five deliveries (registered 117B to 121B) in March of that year. A further 17 armoured cars were delivered in July 1941, while a further 80 chassis were waiting to be fitted with turrets. For technical data, please refer to the first page and the final information sheet.

■ ARMAMENT

We dwell on the armament of the AB40 because it is essentially the issue that most differentiates it from the model to follow, the AB41. The armament consisted of three Breda Model 38 8mm machine guns. These had 24 curved round magazines. This machine gun was directly derived from the famous Breda Mod. 37 infantry machine gun. Two machine guns were twin-mounted at the front of the turret. Their maximum elevation was +18° while the lowering was -9°. The third machine gun was positioned on the right side of the vehicle, looking backwards, and was positioned on a ball mount that offered greater horizon spacing. The rear machine gun could also be dismounted and mounted on an anti-aircraft mount on the turret roof, the same mount already used on the 'M' series tanks.

▲ An AB 40 with twin turret machine gun in the Ansaldo production warehouses, 1939.

AUTOBLINDO AB41, NORTH AFRICA 1942

▲ Fiat Ansaldo AB41 armoured car in Libya. Belonging to the 3rd Armoured Group 'Nice', 1st Squadron, 4th Platoon, spring 1942 Libya.

■ AB42

In 1941, the Regio Esercito realised that the performance of its albeit reliable and modern AB41 armoured car could not meet the operational requirements of the African Campaign. A design was therefore considered that could meet the shortcomings demonstrated in the theatre of operations. It was therefore thought to modify the AB41 to better suit its use in North Africa. Thus was born the AB42, a lighter and faster aircraft, of which, however, only one prototype was eventually produced in 1942. Its early end was mainly due to the changed wartime situation that became apparent at the end of 1942, when the North African campaign turned against the Axis forces and a long-range reconnaissance vehicle with the characteristics of the AB42 was no longer needed.

Fortunately, some of the systems developed for the AB42 were reused on the AB43, the next armoured car, which retained the AB41's chassis and superstructure but had the new, more powerful engine and turret of the Light Armoured Car Mod. 1942.

A 42-command Autoblindo was also designed: without turret, retreating machine gun and double guide used as a command post (it was ordered in 50 examples but apparently never delivered).

■ AB WITH 47/32 CANNON

Armoured car with 47/32 gun: hypothesised to be able to take on the most heavily armed enemy scout units, it mounted the 47/32 gun and had no secondary armament. It was never adopted and remained at the prototype stage (see profile on p. 26).

■ AB RAILWAY

For use on rails by the railway engineers. In this model with road tyres replaced with those used for railways (see profile on p. 28).

For the railway model, AB 40 and 41 were used for a total number of about 20 units. These vehicles were prepared in 1942 to patrol the Yugoslav railways. This special version was called 'Railway'. After the war, another group of AB41 and AB43 vehicles was modified for the same purpose but to be used for patrolling Italian railways.

▲ A railway AB 40 with steel wheels on rails. This is a prototype version of the AB Ferroviaria from the FIAT factory. The spare wheels, in addition to the fixing pins, were supported by a steel cable that was hooked to the superstructure when not in use.

AUTOBLINDO AB42, NORTH AFRICA 1942

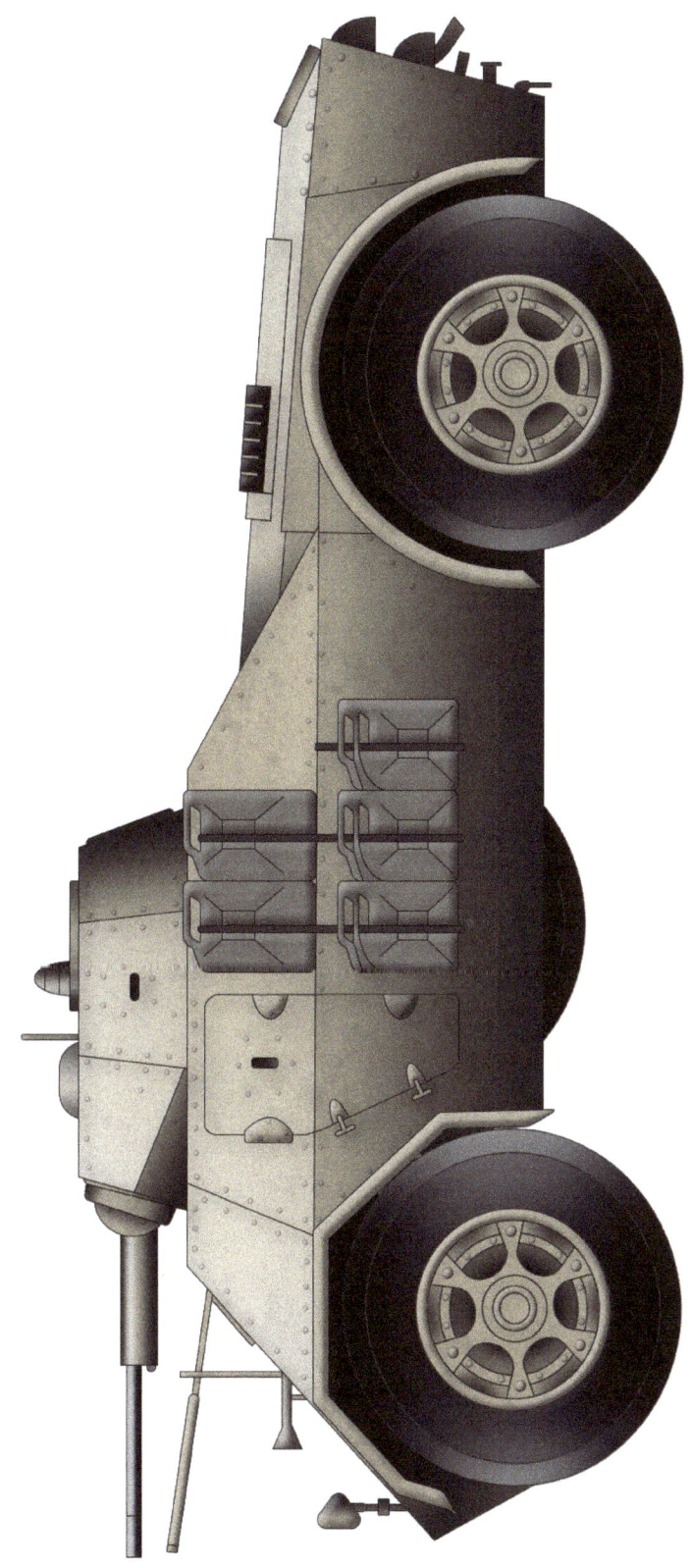

▲ AB42 armoured car. Developed only in prototype terms, it served essentially to refine the future AB43.

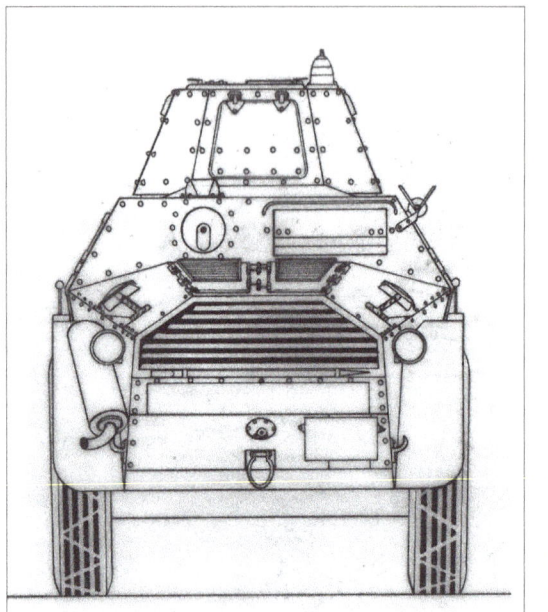
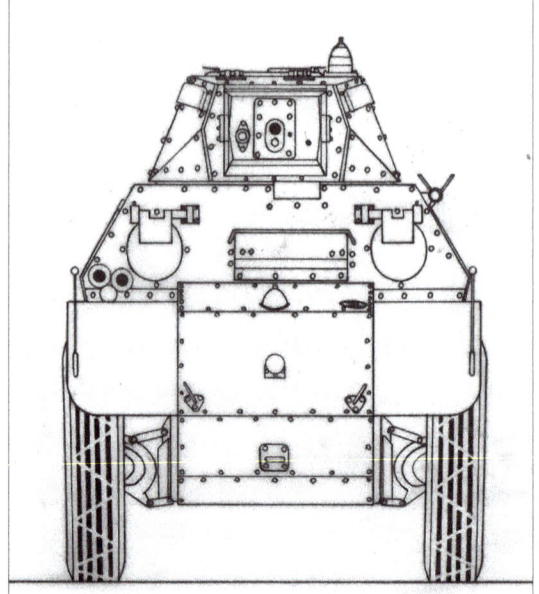
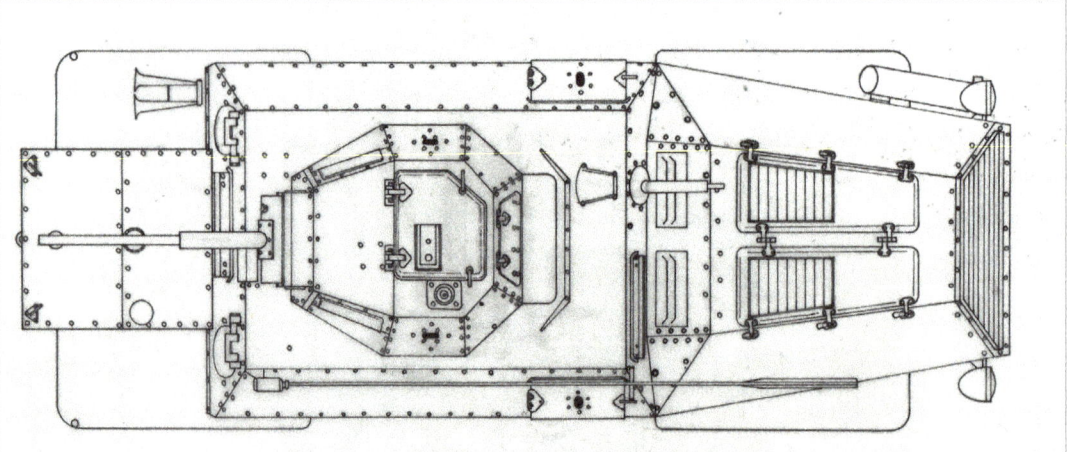

▲▼ AB 41 armoured car profiles designed by Roberto Vela (courtesy of Roberto Vela).

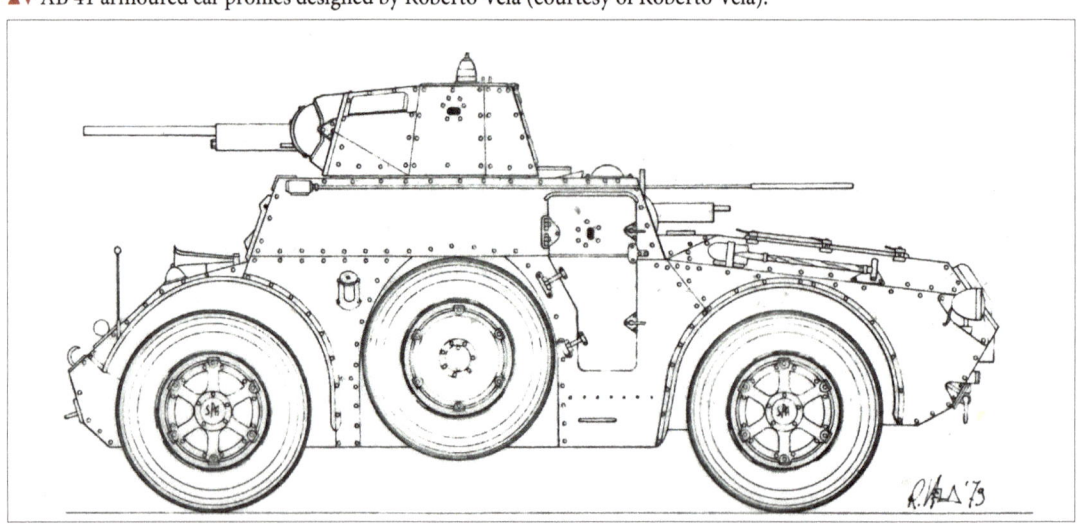

AUTOBLINDO AB41, LYBIA 1941

▲ AB41 armoured car in Libya. Armed with a 20mm Breda cannon. This vehicle belonged to the Tank Instruction Centre in North Africa.

AUTOBLINDO AB41, NORTH AFRICA 1942

▲ AB41 armoured car in Africa. This is the famous 'disputed' armoured car between the CXXXII NEC and the enemy allied unit of the 'Carpathaina lancers' who captured the vehicle during operations in the desert.

AB41 AND AB43

■ **AB41**

The Italian High Command soon realised that the two machine guns in the turret mounted on the AB40 could not provide adequate infantry support fire and, more importantly, did not allow the AB40 to engage even similar enemy vehicles. Ansaldo therefore proposed to install a new turret on the AB40's chassis; they immediately thought of the one already developed for the L6/40 light tank, armed with a 20 mm automatic cannon. Thus was born the AB41 armoured car, destined to be the most produced of the series. The modifications increased the total weight of the vehicle from 6.8 to 7.45 tonnes. This led in turn to the need for a more powerful petrol engine, the FIAT SPA ABM 2 6-cylinder 88-horsepower engine. After some tests, the new vehicle was judged favourably by the army, which authorised its production. After a short time, the new Model 1941 turrets, already in production for the L6/40, arrived on the assembly lines. However, the new engines were not as available in the short term, so it was decided to modify the AB40 armoured cars by fitting the Model 41 turret with the old engine. These 'hybrid' armoured cars were indistinguishable from the AB41 from the outside.

The new turret

The L6/40's single-seat turret was octagonal in shape and had two hatches: one located on the roof for the vehicle's commander/ gunner, and a second at the rear, useful for facilitating the removal of the main armament during maintenance operations. On either side of the turret were two louvers and two air intakes, as the vehicle had neither fans nor smoke extractors. On the roof, next to the hatch, there was a periscope that allowed the commander a partial view of the battlefield, which was limited by the impossibility of rotating it 360° due to the confined space. In time, there were balance problems in the turret, which were solved by adding a counterweight at the rear, under the rear hatch.

▲ An AB41 operating in the Libyan desert at Bir el Gobi. Note the large Italian flag painted on the side, soon to be replaced with a white circle on the turret roof for enemy aircraft recognition.

The 20/65 Breda cannon

Obviously, the AB41's main change from the previous model was the replacement of the two twin machine guns in the turret. The main armament consisted of the good 20/65 Breda Mod. 1935 cannon already in use on the L/65, with a firing rate of 220 rounds per minute and a sight manufactured by Ottica San Giorgio. The elevation of the cannon was +18° while the depression was -9°. This cannon could fire Italian-made armour-piercing (AP) and high-explosive (HE) projectiles, calibre 20 x 138 mm, in addition to those used by the German FlaK 38 cannon and the Soletta S18-1000 anti-tank cannon, thus greatly enhancing its anti-tank capabilities. Using Italian armour-piercing shells, the Mod. 1935 was able to penetrate a 38 mm shell inclined at 90° at a distance of 100 metres, and a 30 mm shell at 500 metres. Using the German Pz.Gr. 40 armour-piercing projectiles, it could penetrate a 50 mm armour at a 90° angle at 100 metres and a 40 mm armour at 500 metres.

The secondary armament, on the other hand, consisted of two Breda Model 1938 8 mm machine guns, the first coaxial to the gun, on the left, and the second, as in the AB40 model, in a spherical mount on the rear of the vehicle. These machine guns were the vehicle version of the Breda Model 1937 medium machine gun and had a top-mounted curved box magazine with 24 rounds.

The machine gun in the rear could be dismantled and used in an anti-aircraft position.

▲ Italian fighters with their AB41 engaged in the African desert, the shape of the radio antenna can be seen very well.

AUTOBLINDO AB41, NORTH AFRICA 1943

▲ AB41 armoured car in Libya. In continental factory camouflage colour.

AUTOBLINDO AB41, NORTH AFRICA 1943

▲ AB41 armoured car in Libya. Self-propelled artillery version with 47mm open-top piece.

26 | TWE

AUTOBLINDO AB40/41/42/43

AB43

The cancellation of the AB42 project due to the Axis defeats in the North African campaign at the end of 1942 led to the development of a new vehicle, the AB43, on the same chassis as the AB41 but with a new turret and a new, more powerful engine. The new vehicle also received new armament and was equipped with a special 47mm semi-automatic cannon in an enlarged and better protected turret. The AB43 was immediately tested but the Royal Italian Army could not start production in time due to the Cassibile Armistice signed on 8 September 1943.

The AB43 represented the latest evolution of the AB40/41 series of armoured vehicles. In 1944, when central-northern Italy was entirely occupied by the German army, which controlled the industrial activities in northern Italy, the latter imposed new production for its own army and assigned the designation '**PzSpWg AB43 203(i)**', allocating this last model to combat activities against Italian and Balkan partisans. Under German leadership, the vehicle was produced in a total of just over 100 units until 1945.

The bodywork of the AB43 did not undergo any major changes compared to that of the AB40/41, consisting of armoured plates riveted to the chassis. Instead, the main novelty consisted of the aforementioned new turret (derived from the M13/40 tank) armed with a Breda 47/32 Mod. 1935 47 mm cannon with 63 rounds. In the AB43 we again find the same Breda Mod.38 8 mm machine guns with 756 rounds each. The engine retains the old Fiat S.P.A petrol engine but with a power output of 108 hp instead of the AB41's 88 hp.

The new turret

The new AB43 armoured car was fitted with the 1942 turret already developed for the AB42 armoured car.

The single-seat turret had an octagonal shape with two hatches: one for the commander/machine gunner on the roof, which was divided into two separate doors, and the second at the rear of the turret, used to facilitate

▲ Column of AB41s on the move in a Tunisian village. In small: AB41 assembly line.

AUTOBLINDO AB40 RAILWAY, BALKANS 1942

▲ AB41 armoured car in railway version with continental colouring. Balkans 1942.

the dismantling of the main armament during maintenance operations. On either side of the turret were two embrasures, and on the roof was the anti-aircraft gun mount, and a periscope for the commander next to the hatch, giving him a full view of the battlefield. Due to the size of the turret, which was only 35 cm high, a protuberance was bolted to the roof of the turret, which held the top-mounted curved box magazine of the Breda Mod 38 coaxial machine gun, allowing the gun to reach an even wider depression.

AB43 'CANNON' WITH 47MM PIECE

The AB43 'Cannon' was a prototype version of the AB armoured car series armed with an anti-tank variant of the standard 47 mm Italian infantry support gun. It was intended to improve the anti-tank and support characteristics of the 'AB' armoured car series.

The only prototype was developed and produced by Ansaldo and FIAT for the Regio Esercito. The AB43 'Cannon' prototype was only allowed to take part in some tests before 8 September 1943, the date on which the Cassibile Armistice was signed, effectively putting Italy out of the war. The prototype that was presented to the Royal Army High Command satisfied the officers involved. As many as 380 AB43 'Cannon' vehicles were ordered, but as mentioned, only the prototype was made.

In the weeks following the armistice, German troops captured the prototype, naming it 'Panzerspähwagen FIAT/SPA Typ AB43(I) mit 4,7 cm kanone im Drehturm', but unlike the standard version of the AB43, this new vehicle was considered of little use by the Germans, so the vehicle was stored and forgotten to rust in the Ansaldo factory warehouses.

The main feature of this new vehicle was, as always, the armament, which consisted of a 47/40 Mod. 1938 cannon. This was of the same type also mounted on the Italian M15/42 medium tank. It was a significantly more powerful cannon than the 47/32 Mod. of the normal AB43, which in turn was already used on the L40 47/32 medium tanks and the M13/40 and M14/41.

▲ The AB41s of the 8th Bersaglieri Battalion with the commanders discussing the mission and ready for action. North African Desert 1942.

AUTOBLINDO AB41, ALBANIA 1943

▲ AB41 armoured car of the 4th 'Nice' Group in service in Albania and the Balkans. Estae 1943.

OPERATIONAL USE

The ABs, although equipped with light armour that made them vulnerable to most weapons, found employment in scout units on all fronts where the Royal Army was engaged: North Africa, where in the AB 4 variant, AOI, in the Balkans, Hungary, France in Russia and Italy. In the Italian army, these vehicles were basically assigned to the cavalry, the Italian Police in Africa (PAI) and the Bersaglieri units. The vehicles were also organised into reconnaissance battalions (or cavalry groups) of three or four companies each. Each armoured car company consisted of three armoured car platoons of four armoured cars each, an armoured car for the company commander and an armoured car for the company headquarters (HQ) for a total of 42 or 56 AB 41 in total. Each independent and fully equipped armoured car company proved itself equal to its assigned tasks of reconnaissance, escort and security. The special rail vehicles were mainly used in anti-partisan patrols in the Balkans.

■ WAR IN NORTH AFRICA 1940-1943

The first armoured cars were assigned at the end of 1941 to RECAM (Raggruppamento Esplorante del Corpo d'Armata di Manovra), which was equipped with an experimental platoon of armoured cars from the Gruppo Squadroni Armorati "Nizza" (Armoured Squadron Group "Nice") due to the very limited number of vehicles assigned to it, it was disbanded in January 1942. In its place was created the RCAS (Raggruppamento Celere Africa Settentrionale), divided into two groups, each consisting of an armoured car squadron with 24 AB41s, a 65/17 Self-Propelled Battery Group, a 75/27 Mod. 11 Self-Propelled Battery Group, a 100/17 Self-Propelled Battery Group and a 20/65 Anti-Aircraft Battery. These units were supported by two infantry battalions and logistics units. It is not clear whether the armoured cars in the unit were from the III Armoured Explorers Group 'Cavalleggeri di Monferrato' of the III Armoured Group 'Nizza'. It is likely that the unit was equipped with some armoured cars from this unit or others.
In May 1942, there were a total of 93 armoured cars in North Africa, assigned to various units:
- The 3rd Armoured Group 'Nizza', with a theoretical organic strength of 47 armoured cars, but equipped with 38 vehicles;
- the 8th Armoured Bersaglieri Regiment, also with a theoretical organic strength of 47 armoured cars;
- The 3rd Company of the Italian African Police, with a theoretical staff of 10;
Subsequently, the 3rd Armoured Expeditionary Group (GECo) 'Cavalleggeri di Monferrato', assigned to the 131st Armoured Division 'Centauro' took part in the occupation of the Jalo Oasis in Cyrenaica, Libya, and then the Siwa Oasis in Egypt, together with the 136th Armoured Division 'Giovani Fascisti'. After the defeat of the Axis troops in the Second Battle of El Alamein, the 3rd Armoured Expeditionary Group 'Cavalleggeri di Monferrato' fought against Allied armoured units in southern Tunisia.
Although it was only a reconnaissance unit, after the end of 1942 it was used to counter attacks by the British Long Range Desert Group (LRDG). It succeeded on one occasion in capturing the commander of the famous British unit, Lieutenant Colonel David Stirling, on 20 January 1943, near Al Hāmmah an oasis in southern Tunisia. During the Battle of Al Hāmmah in March 1943, he actively participated in the retreat from the Kebili area, fighting against Free French forces and British guards.
All remaining armoured units in Tunisia, including the 3rd Armoured Expeditionary Group 'Cavalleggeri di Monferrato', fought in the defence of Cape Bon until the surrender of the Axis troops in Tunisia on 13 May 1943.
Another unit that made a name for itself in Africa and equipped with ABs was the 'Cavalleggeri di Lodi' Armoured Expeditionary Regiment. Already destined for the Russian front, by order of the Royal Army General Staff, on 19 September, the destination was moved to North Africa, to the XX Manoeuvre Army Corps, for the defence of the Libyan Sahara. A key role that Italian scout units played in Libya and Tunisia was to counter enemy scout units, in order to interfere with enemy intelligence gathering. The ABs also came in useful in anti-aircraft roles, shooting down a Lockheed P-38 Lightning, a Bristol Beaufighter and an American four-engine aircraft. Two American fighters were also shot down at Mezzauna by a platoon

of 20 mm automatic anti-aircraft guns and a platoon of armoured cars fought against enemy armoured vehicles near Krechen.

During the Battle of the Kasserine Pass, all units of the Armoured Expeditionary Regiment 'Lodi Cavalry' were engaged, from the preliminary operations until the end of the offensive. In collaboration with the 21st. Panzer Division occupied the Kralif, Rabeau and Faid passes, the starting point of the Sidi Bou Zid attack. Then followed the inevitable retreat until 11 May 1943, when after fighting north-west of Boufichia, what was left of the RECo was annihilated in bitter fighting that resulted in the destruction of the unit's last armoured artillery vehicles.

Other Italian AB-armoured units active in Africa were the 3rd Armoured Group 'Lancieri di Novara', the 3rd Armoured Group 'Nizza' and the 8th Armoured Bersaglieri Battalion 'Autonomo'.

■ CONTINENTAL OPERATION

The 18th Bersaglieri Armoured Regiment was active in France and the 10th Bersaglieri Celere Regiment in Corsica, which was created on 1 February 1942. The 18th RECo Bersaglieri had the 1st Autoblindo Company with 17 AB41 armoured cars at its disposal.

On 3rd January 1943, the 18th RECo Bersaglieri was assigned to the 4th Italian Army deployed in Provence, with garrison duties near Toulon, in view of possible enemy landings. On 25 July 1943, the regiment returned to Turin, but the 1st Armoured Company, renamed 7th Company, went to reinforce the 10th Bersaglieri Celere Regiment in Corsica. There it was used to patrol Corsica's coastal roads to prevent partisan attacks and to monitor the Mediterranean Sea. After the armistice of 8 September 1943, the company took part in the fighting against the 16. SS-Panzergrenadier-Division "Reichsführer-SS". After 25 September 1943, the Free French troops arrived on the island and sided with the Italians. On 29 September the Franco-Italian offensive against the Germans began and was successful. The Germans were forced to hastily re-embark from Bastia for the mainland. By 5 October all Germans had fled or surrendered. The French confiscated heavy weapons from the Italian units.

▲ Two AB41s of the 18th Bersaglieri Armoured Scout Regiment during training in Corsica. The vehicles had some canisters on the rear of the turret.

▲ A crew member of the 18th Bersaglieri cleans a Breda Model 1938 on the turret of his AB41.

▼ Two AB41s of the III Armoured Expeditionary Group 'Cavalleggeri di Monferrato' in North Africa. The two vehicles have no coats of arms.

▲ Two of the three AB41s and the TL37 armoured car assigned to the Army Manoeuvre Corps Exploring Regiment at Sidi Rezegh in November 1941. Visible The motto of the 'Nice' Armoured Squadron Group. State Archives.

▲ Above and to the side: two pictures of Italian AB41 tankers in North Africa from the army magazine: Cronache di Guerra of 1943. Clearly visible anti-aircraft support.

Instead, a cavalry regiment was sent to Albania: the 'Lancieri di Firenze' created on 1 February 1942 and assigned to the 2nd Celere Division 'Emanuele Filiberto Testa di Ferro'. On 10 March 1942, the unit was sent to Albania without armoured cars but equipped with horses. The armoured cars were transferred in July 1942 to the Armoured Exploring Regiment 'Lancieri di Montebello'.

Other units operated in Italy such as the XL Battaglione Bersaglieri Corazzato (Armoured Bersaglieri Battalion) used as an AB training unit in Pinerolo. And again the 'Cavalleggeri di Lucca' motorised regiment stationed in Emilia and then in Rome with public order tasks.

Finally, let us remember the 10th Armoured Exploring Battalion of the 10th Motorized Infantry Division 'Piave' that took part in the desperate defence of Rome in September 1943, defending the northern part of the city. Another unit present in Rome was the 'Lancieri di Montebello' Armoured Exploring Regiment.

▲ Egypt 1941, some AB41s on the Marmarica front near Sidi Barrani.

▲ Two AB41s of the 'Lancieri di Montebello' Armoured Exploring Regiment were hit by German 4.2 cm anti-tank guns. It should be noted that the Italian crews preferred to attack the enemy with the armoured car backwards, to use the engine for protection.

RUSSIA

The only known unit in Russia was the Autonomous Armoured Vehicle Platoon incorporated with the 156th Infantry Division 'Vicenza'. Equipped with only two AB41 armoured cars, these vehicles were used together with some L6/40 light tanks and L40 47/32 self-propelled guns, but were probably soon abandoned due to mechanical wear and tear.

GREECE AND THE BALKANS

12 AB41 armoured cars were handed over to the 9th Autonomous Armoured Car Company, which was assigned to the 11th Italian Army in Greece, as the 8th Autonomous Armoured Car Company. On 31 August 1943, it was disbanded and the 12 armoured cars with their crews were assigned to the Royal Carabinieri General Command, which commanded the Aegean Autonomous Carabinieri Group.

The 8th Autonomous Armoured Car Company with 12 AB41 armoured cars was created in June 1943. It was to be sent to Montenegro but, due to the need for armoured vehicles to patrol and escort convoys to Greece, the unit was eventually handed over to the Italian 11th Army in Greece.

While in the Balkans, some AB41s were handed over to other Italian units. Two AB41s were handed over in May 1942 to the Colonna Celere Confinaria 'M' of the Rijeka Prefecture and one AB41 to the Milizia Nazionale Portuaria. but it was the 4th Armoured Group 'Nizza' that was the largest unit equipped with AB41s on the Yugoslav front. It was part of the Celere Regiment. It was employed in counter-partisan operations and as column escort. After the Armistice of September 1943, they had bloody battles against the Germans, particularly at Burreli and Kruya. After the battle, the 4th Armoured Group 'Nice' dispersed. Many officers and soldiers returned to Italy, reaching their homeland by makeshift means. As already mentioned, a total of 20 AB40s and AB41s in the 'Railway' version were deployed to Yugoslavia to prevent partisan sabotage of railway lines in the Balkans.

AUTOBLINDO AB41 TIRANA, ALBANIA 1943

▲ AB41 armoured car, also belonging to the Armoured Group 'Nice' stationed in Tirana, Albania, until the armistice of 8 September 1943. Equipped with a curious camouflage, this vehicle also bears the department's coat of arms.

AUTOBLINDO AB41, TUNISIA, SPRING 1943

▲ AB41 armoured car of the Regio Esercito, armoured regiment "Cavalleggeri di Lodi", 1st squadron, 2nd platoon, Tunisia, spring 1943.

PARTISANS AND COBELLIGERENT UNITS

Some rare surviving AB41s of the Republican National Army and Republican National Guard were captured or destroyed in the cities of Milan and Turin on 25 April 1945. After the German and Italian surrender, two or three of them took part in the partisan parade in Turin. One of these was used and belonged to the 'San Giusto' Armoured Squadron Group, which was found in the Mairano depot and was taken by the partisans and used against the German garrison in Cividale del Friuli on 28 April 1945. It also participated in an attack against the city of Udine on 30 April.

After the armistice, the Esercito Cobelligerante Italiano was born under Allied command. Among its units, the IX Assault Battalion of the Italian Liberation Corps or CIL had three AB41 armoured cars in service from July 1944. These were used to liberate several towns in the Italian region of Marche. While the 'F' Squadron, composed of Italian soldiers from the British 6th Armoured Division, was equipped after March 1944 with an AB41 platoon consisting of four armoured cars.

GERMAN AB

After 8 September 1943, the Germans occupied all factory assembly lines in north-central Italy and captured most of the remaining Italian vehicles. Around 200 AB41 armoured cars were requisitioned, 20 were captured still at the factory and 23 were produced for the German army, where they were renamed Panzerspähwagen AB41 201(i). A small number of AB41s were transferred to the National Republican Army, while the Germans kept the few AB43s that were highly valued by German crews. In German service, the AB41 was used by the Waffen-SS, Luftwaffe, Wehrmacht and Todt Organisation divisions, serving in France, Germany, Italy and the Balkans. In the Balkans, they were used in anti-partisan operations and airport patrols.

▲ AB41 in German service after the armistice of 8 September 1943. Present on the Balkan front.

▲ An AB41 with desert tyres in Albania, 1942. The need to stem the threat of Tito's partisans was so pressing that many ABs were diverted to Yugoslavia instead of replacing losses in North Africa.

▼ An AB41 turret with counterweight and open rear hatch for mounting the cannon.

▲ Some AB41s during a patrol looking for enemy targets. On the side of the first armoured car was painted a man wearing a rifleman's hat. Above: column of Italian AB41s in Yugoslavia (Bundesarchiv).

AUTOBLINDO AB43 IN GERMAN SERVICE, 1943

▲ Armoured car AB43 captured by German forces and recalled Pz.Sp.Wg. AB43 203 (i).

▲ Parade of AB41s belonging to post-war police departments.

▼ An AB of the PAI with the engine compartment open and the engine extracted and positioned close to the vehicle. North Africa, winter 1942.

AUTOBLINDO AB43, NORTHERN ITALY 1943-1954

▲ AB43 armoured car recently restaurated by Fabio Temeroli, equipped with the long experimental gun.

▲ Exterior of the AB43 armoured car on display at the Militaria exhibition in Novegro. Photo by the author.

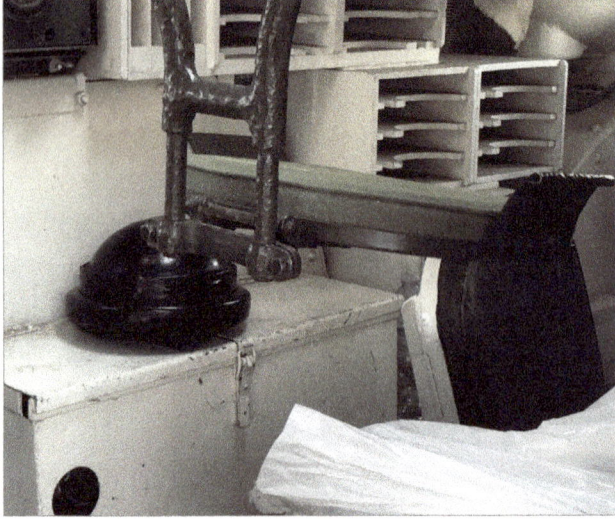

▲ Interior of the AB43 armoured car on display at the Militaria exhibition in Novegro. Photo by the author.

AUTOBLINDO AB43 FLYING "NELLO" ITALY 1944

▲ AB43 armoured car without turret belonging to the Volante 'Nello' in northern Italy.

AUTOBLINDO AB41 FRIULI, ITALY, SETPTEMBER 1944

▲ AB41 SPA-Ansaldo Fossati armoured car, belonging to the 'San Giusto' Armoured Squadron Group, Mariano del Friuli, September 1944.

CAMOUFLAGE AND DISTINCTIVE SIGNS

The background colours of the Autoblindos, from their creation until 1945, (the operational period of this use is indicated in brackets) also used for all armoured vehicles were: R.E. grey green (1936-1945), dark chocolate (1936-1941), reddish brown (1936-1943), ochre (for prototypes), sand (1941-1945), dark sand (1943-1945), dark grey (1941-1943). For camouflage, medium green (1936-1943) and dark red (for prototypes) were used.

National territory 1936-1940 - substantial prevalence of grey-green.
Occupation of Albania and the French Front 1939-1940 - grey-green.
Campaign in Greece and Yugoslavia 1940-1941 - grey-green possibly camouflaged with green and sand-coloured specks.
East Africa 1940-1941 - grey green or in the old Ethiopian campaign camouflage reddish brown with green spots.
North Africa 1940-1943 - at first only grey-green, the colour in which they were generally landed at destination ports, then sand colour in various variegated versions. Not used in the Russian Campaign 1941-1943.
RSI 1943-1945 dark sand colour, reddish brown with medium dense green speckling, in uniform German panzer grey colour. In particular, the tanks of the 'Leonessa' and partly also the 'Leoncello' and 'San Giusto' were dark sand-coloured. I also report the presence of elaborate camouflage in irregular chequered patterns with a sandy yellow background and green and brown patches
Police corps until 1952 dark brick red background colour.
Specific armoured car camouflage: The prototypes were painted at the factory with a so-called 'imperial' livery consisting of a series of relatively thin dark green and dark brown streaks applied over a background of light Saharan khaki, known in Italy as sand colour. This livery was never adopted for the production examples, which were instead painted in a slightly lighter shade of Saharan khaki than that used for the armoured vehicles. If destined for Africa, the vehicles appear to have remained in their colour scheme or repainted once they arrived at their destination in similar colours, while vehicles for continental use often wore factory-applied or circumstantial camouflage schemes. Instead, the last AB 41s and most of the AB 43s left the factory with a rather complex three-tone camouflage livery that included green and reddish-brown patches interspersed with sand-coloured streaks.

■ **MEDIUM, LIGHT AND ARMOURED CAR BADGES**

In order to recognise individual armoured vehicles in military operations, even for Italy, it became necessary to introduce an identification system, also because at least in the beginning there were no tanks with radio equipment installed. In fact, radios only began to be installed with some regularity from 1941 onwards. In the beginning, flags with red or white drapes were used for communication. The first table of distinctive tank markings dates back to 1925 and was very complex and articulated to

excess. Number groups were only introduced in 1927 after the establishment of the Tank Regiment, and new regulations were issued in 1928. In 1940, the first deliveries of M13/40 tanks finally began, which were distributed to the various armoured divisions.

The armoured cars, as had already been the case with the medium or light tanks, bore symbols identified by markings, names and numbers placed on the sides of the hull on both sides. The numbers were painted on the front of the hull plate and on both sides.

In 1938, in order to simplify recognition, a further change was made, this time a radical one: new tactical symbols were established for the tanks. This system was also followed by the armoured cars that came into being a few years later. The vehicle companies were represented by coloured rectangles as follows:

The first company had the colour red, the 2nd^a blue, the 3rd^a yellow, the 4th^a green; white was reserved for the regimental command vehicles. The insignia of the tanks and armoured cars had to be 20 x 12 cm in size and painted in the company colour.

The coloured rectangles were cut by white bars (1 to 4 rows and a diagonal for 5th platoon) and indicated the different platoons, full colour and without rows for Company Command tanks.

The rectangles of the various platoons were surmounted by an Arabic number (the colour of the company) indicating the tank in the platoon's organic formation.

These numbers had to be 10 cm high and 1.5 cm thick, and placed in the centre of the upper side of the rectangle 2 cm apart. Below the rectangle the number of the battalion to which it belonged was placed in white Roman numerals. The battalion tanks, if in reserve at Regimental level, bore instead only the relative Arabic number. Battalion command squadron tanks had a completely black rectangle. The battalion command tank on two companies had it half red and half blue (right). The battalion command tank on three companies had it on three coloured lines from left to right: red, blue and yellow. Specifically for the medium-sized tanks, the badge was placed on the turret in the middle front part. At the rear, in the middle part of the turret. On some tanks, the rectangle was placed at the height of the access hatch to the combat chamber. On the same hatch, the distinctive sign of the Division, such as a black ram, often appeared. The medium-sized tanks used by the Italian Social Republic showed the distinctive signs of the various divisions painted on them: the 'Leoncello' was depicted by a black lion clutching a fascio littorio looking to the left on a white background. The 'Leonessa' had a slightly more complicated distinguishing mark consisting of the red M of Mussolini, cut by a black fascio and underneath the inscription always in black 'GNR'.

The vehicles used by the Germans, especially the captured ones, and the new ones ordered after the armistice in 1943 bore the typical German army markings starting with the black and white *ritterkreuz* in its various guises.

Specifically for armoured cars, Regulation No. 4640 stated that:
- The distinctive sign was to be affixed in the turret, in the centre of the rear plate figure and
laterally - left and right - in the centre of the figure of the plates adjacent to the front plate.
- The Roman and Arabic numerals indicating Sqd (or Btg) and Rgt. should be placed on the side
right of the rear sheet metal of the fighting cabin, in the centre of the surface figure,
right and left respectively, of the retreating machine gun.

Despite the fact that these regulations stipulated that: 'Other badges (name, number group, etc.) on the outside of the tanks, apart from those strictly prescribed by regulations, are forbidden'. In reality, things turned out differently, and in practice, free interpretations of the regulations were adopted.

Such badges were, however, carried on the sides of the superstructure and at the front on the mudguard. In Africa, such badges were often carried larger to ensure greater visibility. In addition, as was already the case for the tanks, again in Africa, from 1941 it became compulsory to wear air recognition devices for the AB, which was the customary white circle 70 cm in diameter painted on the outside of the turret top. Prior to this, as is well shown in some pictures of 'Nice' armoured cars and other Italian vehicles mistakenly ran into attacks by our planes and bombers or the Axis in general.

At first, huge coloured tricolour flags were used on the front and sides of the vehicles. then the aforementioned white circle was used.

▲ Replacing a 'Claw' tyre on an AB41 of the 4th Armoured Group 'Nice' stationed in Tirana, Albania. Photo taken before the Armistice. Source piciuki.com

AUTOBLINDO AB41, GERMAN USE 1944

▲ AB41 armoured car reused by the Wehrmacht, specifically the 162nd Infantry Division, Italy, July 1944.

▲▼ AB41 in the possession of RSI units, above the GNR of the Leonessa armoured group (Archive Borgatti) and below battalion IX September (Archive Viziano).

AUTOBLINDO AB41, RSI ITALY, APRIL 1945

▲ AB41 armoured car belonging to the XI September Group, RSI, Italy, April 1945.

PRODUCTION AND EXPORT

Many Italian companies took part in the ambitious project and production of the 'AB' series armoured cars:
- The SPA (Società Piemontese Automobili di Torino) produced the chassis and engines;
- Lancia in Turin also produced a small percentage of chassis;
- San Giorgio in Sestri Ponente near Genoa produced all the optical devices for the armoured car;
- Milan company Magneti Marelli took charge of the radio system, batteries and engine start-up;
- The armour plates were produced by Società Italiana Acciaierie Cornigliano or SIAC;
- The Società Italiana Ernesto Breda per Costruzioni Meccaniche in Brescia supplied the armament, namely the automatic cannons and machine guns;
- At Ansaldo-Fossati in Sestri-Ponente they assembled the hull and produced the turrets.

Altogether more than 700 of all types were produced. In the ten months of 1941, during which the AB41, the most produced of the models, was produced, 250 were delivered to the army, instead of the 300 insured. to be precise, between frames and superstructures around 270.

The following year, 1942, 302 AB41 armoured cars were delivered to the army, also with an average monthly production of 25. In 1943, due to various problems, only 72 were delivered to the army between January and July, and these were also the last. Under the German Generalinspekteur der Panzertruppen, after the armistice signed by the Italians with the Allies in the winter of 1943, production was resumed after positive assessments by the Germans for the Wehrmacht and reached a total of 23 AB41s produced until December 1944.

Major users

Italy: as always, the main user was the country of origin of the vehicle. the number of orders and deliveries that took place has already been indicated.
Operational mainly in the North African theatre and the Balkans, in various versions. Less so the special version, known as the Ferroviaria, which was mainly used in the Balkans together with the armed trains of the Regio Esercito in anti-partisan activities.
REI's last deployment took place during the battle for the German conquest of Rome, with some units deployed to defend the capital from the Italian military. The vehicles were almost destroyed in combat at Montagnola on the Via Laurentina by German paratroopers on 10 September 1943.

Germany: as happened with all Italian weapons that fell into German hands following the armistice of September 1943, and the subsequent collapse and surrender of the units to the German armed forces, many ABs also became part of their equipment. Not only that, in 1944, the Germans, who occupied the northern industries, restarted production by adopting the vehicle under the new name PzSpWg AB43 203(i), then assigning the new vehicles to Wehrmacht units engaged in anti-partisan combat. Probably also for these second-line tasks, the armament was reduced to the usual 20 mm Breda, but this time in a slightly lower turret. A further model produced for the German forces was equipped with a 50mm cannon (to suit German ammunition) and an uncovered body.

Italy RSI: The Wehrmacht took it upon itself to supply the formations of the Republic of Salò with some armoured cars, especially as an anti-guerrilla warfare measure.

Italy Republic: In the post-war period, the few surviving units were assigned to the State Police's rapid response units, remaining in the force until the early 1950s.

AUTOBLINDO AB41 POLICE SERVICE, ITALY 1951

▲ AB41 armoured car in service with the state police's rapid response units. In typical dark brick red colouring. Italian Republic 1951

DATA SHEET AB40/41/43	
Dimensions	5.2 x 1.92 width x 2.48 height in m
Weight	6,85 t
Crew	4
Engine	SPA ABM in-line 6-cylinder, petrol-driven.
Maximum road speed	76 kilometres per hour. 38km off road
Autonomy	400 km AB40/41 and 350 km AB43
Suspension	independent four-wheel steering
Armament	-Two twin 8 mm Breda Mod. 38 machine guns (AB40). -Breda 20/65 Mod. 1935 20 mm cannon (AB41). - 47/32 Mod. 1935 47 mm cannon (AB43).
Secondary armament	-Breda Mod. 38 8-mm machine gun in casemate (all models), -Breda Mod. 38 8 mm coaxial turret gun (AB41 and AB43)
Setting date	1938, 1941 and 1943
Production	AB40: 24, AB41: 600, AB43: 70
Users	Italy REI, Italy RSI, Germany, post-WWII Italy

▲ Three images of AB41s operating in North Africa. State Archives.

BIBLIOGRAPHY

- Nicola Pignato, *Storia dei mezzi corazzati*, Fratelli Fabbri editori, 1976, pp. 81-88.
- A.Bruschi, M.Biava, *Autoblindo AB41 e AB43*. Auriga Publishing 2005
- Bruno Benvenuti e Ugo F. Colonna - *L'armamento italiano nella seconda guerra mondiale Carri armati in servizio fra le due guerre 1* - Edizioni Bizzarri, Roma 1972
- Maurizio Parri, *Tracce di cingolo - compendio di generale di storia dei carristi 1919-2009*, Assocarri, 2009
- Filippo Cappellano, *Autoblindo AB 40, 41 e 43. Tecnica e storia dei più celebri blindati ruotati italiani della seconda guerra mondiale.* Albertelli 2011
- Filippo Cappellano, *Gli autoveicoli da combattimento dell'Esercito Italiano, vol.1*, Ufficio Storico dello Stato Maggiore dell'Esercito, Roma 2002.
- N.Pignato e F. D'Inzeo, *Le autoblindo AB40, 41 e 43*. Gli appunti di Modellismo più
- S.M.R.E. - *"Nozioni di armi, tiro e materiali vari"*, Edizioni Le "Forze Armate", Roma, 1942.
- N. Pignato, *"I mezzi blindo-corazzati italiani 1923-1943"*, Albertelli Edizioni Speciali, Parma, 2004.
- Ralph E Jones, George H Rarey, Robert J. Icks: *The fighting Tanks since 1916.*
- John Joseph Timothy Sweet, *Iron Arm: The Mechanization of Mussolini's Army, 1920-1940*, Stackpole Books, 2007
- Emiliano Ciaralli *Le Forze Armate, 1935* – Colonel Pederzini, *Italian Tanks 1917-1945.*
- Nico Sgarlato *Corazzati Italiani 1939-1945*, War Set n°10, 2006.
- David Vannucci, *Corazzati e blindati italiani dalle origini allo scoppio della seconda guerra mondiale*, Editrice Innocenti, 2003.
- Daniele Guglielmi, *Autoblindo AB 41 & AB 43 Italian Armored Cars (Armor PhotoGallery, Volume 8)*. Model Centrum Progres (January 1, 2004)
- Daniele Guglielmi & David Zambon, *Les véhicules blindés italiens 1910/43 (1ère partie)*, Batailles & Blindés n°24, 2008.
- Lucio Ceva & Andrea Curami, *La meccanizzazione dell'esercito dalle origini al 1943, Tomo II*, USSME, 1994
- Ugo Barlozzetti & Alberto Pirella *Mezzi dell'Esercito Italiano 1935-45*, Editoriale Olimpia, 1986
- Ralph Riccio, Marcello Calzolari e Nicola Pignato, *Italian Tanks and Combat Vehicles of World War II*, Roadrunner Mattioli, 2010
- Alberto Pirella, *Autoblindo dell'asse: autoblindo italo-tedesche 1920 - 1945*, Ciarrapico 1977
- Paolo Crippa e Carlo Cucut *I reparti corazzati italiani nei Balcani*, Soldiershop 2019.
- Paolo Crippa. *I reparti corazzati del R.E. E l'armistizio 1° Volume*, Soldiershop 2021.
- Paolo Crippa. *I reparti corazzati del R.E. E l'armistizio 2° Volume*, Soldiershop 2021.

PUBLISHED TITLES

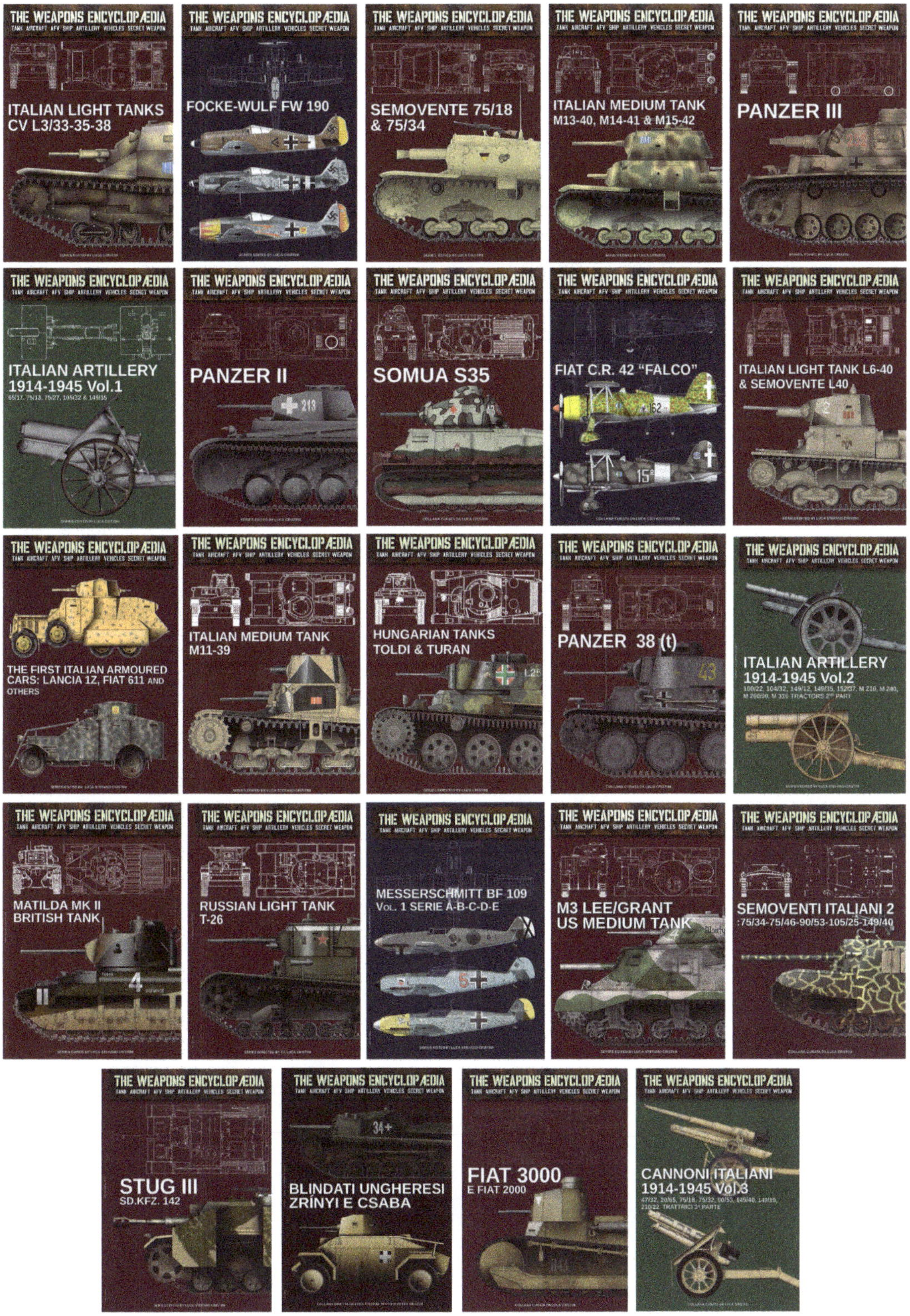
THE WEAPONS ENCYCLOPÆDIA
ITALIAN LIGHT TANKS CV L3/33-35-38
FOCKE-WULF FW 190
SEMOVENTE 75/18 & 75/34
ITALIAN MEDIUM TANK M13-40, M14-41 & M15-42
PANZER III
ITALIAN ARTILLERY 1914-1945 Vol.1
PANZER II
SOMUA S35
FIAT C.R. 42 "FALCO"
ITALIAN LIGHT TANK L6-40 & SEMOVENTE L40
THE FIRST ITALIAN ARMOURED CARS: LANCIA 1Z, FIAT 611 AND OTHERS
ITALIAN MEDIUM TANK M11-39
HUNGARIAN TANKS TOLDI & TURAN
PANZER 38 (t)
ITALIAN ARTILLERY 1914-1945 Vol.2
MATILDA MK II BRITISH TANK
RUSSIAN LIGHT TANK T-26
MESSERSCHMITT BF 109 Vol. 1 SERIE A-B-C-D-E
M3 LEE/GRANT US MEDIUM TANK
SEMOVENTI ITALIANI 2 :75/34-75/46-90/53-105/25-149/40
STUG III SD.KFZ. 142
BLINDATI UNGHERESI ZRINYI E CSABA
FIAT 3000 E FIAT 2000
CANNONI ITALIANI 1914-1945 Vol.3

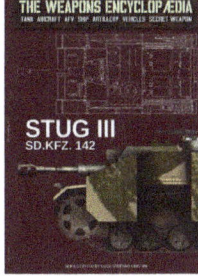

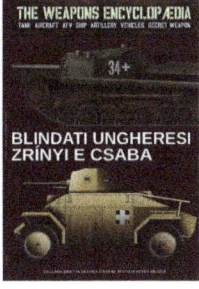

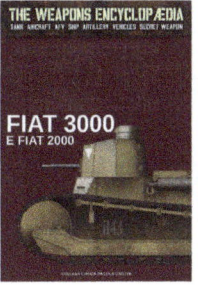

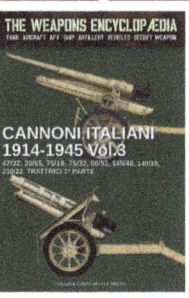

TWE-027 EN

www.ingramcontent.com/pod-product-compliance
Lightning Source LLC
LaVergne TN
LVHW072121060526
838201LV00068B/4942